i

Cedro

The Dog Who Served His Backyard
With Distinction

Cedro

The Dog Who Served His Backyard
With Distinction

Megan Baldrige

Jules' Poetry Playhouse Publications

Albuquerque, NM

For Cedro,

*and for all the unsung dogs who befriend and serve dog-lovers,
with distinction.*

And also for Diego, Jack, Fonda and Malcolm.

All of you inspire me, wordfully, always.

Cover drawing: Fonda Carranza

Cover design: Denise Weaver Ross and Jules Nyquist

Acknowledgements

"A Dry, Dusty Dog" appeared in the *Bosque Beast*, September, 2015

Back cover quotes: http://dogtime.com/dog-health/general/ 16344-25-famous-quotes-about- dogs#l3LHFpXh9Whf70q8.99

ISBN-13: 978-1976514258
ISBN-10: 1976514258

Preface

In 2006, a casual jaunt with my son Jack to the dog shelter turned into a tumultuous ten-year friendship with an irascible, disobedient Black Lab-Chow named Cedro—after a mountain peak near our house in Cedar Crest, New Mexico.

In the next few years, my family dispersed, due to divorce and four children's moves on to college.

Cedro and I continued as a family of two who walked together every day, but experienced the world in distinctly different ways.

Cedro lived in the moment, and prejudged others strongly by a codified system of judgement: raccoons, poodles and cats were unworthy of respect.

Ducks were fair game and Labradoodles were not poodles. Despite many discussions with him about his rush to judge, he never budged an inch.

Despite our mutual affection, we challenged each other daily. We each benefitted from our great friendship and we each came to understand the other's point of view, without ever agreeing.

As is true of most dogs with big hearts, Cedro's life was too short.

These poems are my attempt to describe, celebrate and understand my great friend.

Megan Baldrige

Albuquerque, NM, October 2017

Table of Contents

1

Dog Wrestling:

Dog Wrestling: An Imperfect Human (Who Likes to Complain) and a Fallible Dog (Who Barks Way Too Much) Duke it out

*watch out for flying bites, growls, vet bills for the other dog, misunderstandings and tears.

Blind Date with a Carnivorous Stranger

At the pound,
I locked eyes
with a sweet-natured,
Buddhalike black lab.

I was smitten
with loving eyes
of chocolate brown
in which I saw pleading:
for life-after-the-pound redemption.

As I read him, he read me:
he ramped up the winsome,
looked at me with hopeful love
I had not yet earned,
put his best paw forward,
to look adorable, adoptable.

We walked quietly
from his cell. He,
omega to my alpha,
wagging his tail thousands of times,
gazing lovingly at my leg,
while I signed him out
for his trial run as my dog.

For the first month,
there were no growls,
no fur shedding,
no cat endangerment,
nor swaggering,

nary a dog hair
on the sofa.

He forsook
digging up the flowerbed;
his 30-day trial ended
in a flurry of kindness.

On the 31st day,
Mr. Alpha smiled at me,
Ms. Beta.
His front snaggle teeth
slid from his mouth,
glinting with satisfaction
amidst undertones of duplicity,
into which I read,
"Thanks for adopting me.
Now that I'm off probation
let me be honest:
I sometimes lounge
on the sofa but don't worry,
never while you are at home."
Thus, we both awoke from his tryout
and the barking-digging chapter officially began.

The Chow In Him Meets the Bulldog in Me

Sometimes we align,
like two peas in a pod,
both of us up early, ready to walk,
me leading, him following.

Sometimes our hierarchy
suffers setbacks:
His dominant gene
not deferring
to my ambivalent leadership.

Unsubmissive to alpha me,
his philosophy of
"Let a dog be a dog"
challenges my mantra:
"You are not our top dog."

In the mythical prelapsarian
environment where canines
roamed freely
we might have shared
alphahood: he the alpha hunter
and me the human visionary.

Nowadays, between us
it's moment-to-moment combat
about who is wearing the alpha pants:
he wrestling to claim
the royal mantle of top dog
I should be clad in.

The alpha in me
has learned vigilance,
so my dog can relax.
I've learned to keep a lookout
down the paths of our walks,
for feral ducks and dogs.

I've learned to mad-dog
my sometimes-mad dog.
And to never give
the alpha mantle up
without a big argument,
and then not to lose the
argument.

The Chow-Lab Mestizo Who Parks His Dog Dish in My Kitchen

He is not a bad dog;
but a dog
who makes *bad choices*.
Throwing caution to the wind
when he sees an unlikeable raccoon,
his animus offended by anotherness
floods his rational parts.
The brain that should say
"Dude you're a suburban house dog
dragging a leash; you cannot chase right now",
instead yells, "Let's show that other dog!"

Undiagnosed by a vet,
he clearly suffers from PTJRSD,
Post-Traumatic Jack Russell Stress Disorder.
When he sees a proud purebred
with attitude,
he flashes back to a rollicking dogfight in the 1960s,
a raw burque rumble,
before animal welfare,
spaying, pet adoption
disbanded dog packs.
He could not have been
at that mythic fight,
but his dog dreams take him there.

He ALSO tries to throw his weight around
when he sees cockapoos
and other mestizos,

forgetting that a mixed-breed coupling.
made him he.

Under stress, chow emotions
overpower his lab heart.
One minute,
he's a black-lab flower child
licking the hands of bosque-walking
three year olds,
all high-fives,
and "Let's-get-together-again-soon."
Next he's a high-alert, guard dog
chomping at the bit, all business,
gruff glare.
"Cuidado, there's a labradoodle headed our way",
he says, hair and 'tude bristling.

On one of our walks, the perfect storm
struck like lightning.
An enemy of provenance, questionable,
approached, not respectfully enough
at the beginning of a walk,
a moment known to be emotionally fragile.

Our shared leash snapped off
my dog's collar,
from the weight of his ceaseless straining.
His desire to be respected unchecked,
he attacked the enemy,
someone else's pet on a leash.

Suddenly his canine teeth
were embedded in the other's neck.
The dog's owner and I discovered
the entanglement
at the same moment, both horrified:
he: at the fragility of life.
the proximity of death
me: at the future vet bill,
lawsuit,
and had I thrown away his rabies paperwork
when I cleaned up my desk?

I think my dog's late chow grandmother
was whispering fight chants in his ear
"You are an ultimate fighting machine"
"Avenge our family"
"Don't let this cur dis you."
"Winner takes all"
or some such doggerel.
I certainly was yelling things like,
"Come back and pick up your leash"
"Don't be doing this for me"
"Remember Vietnam"
"Remember Superbowl XLVIII"
"Remember the Alamo"
"You are not Caesar"
"Watch out for that dog's teeth"
"Avoid his neck,"
none of which he was listening to.

Later at dinner
the loving lab approached me
plaintively courting pats,
as the cocky chow licked his wounds,
swishing away the blood
of another injured soul.

My Low-Water Usage Dog

Poet Laureate Billy Collins
writes in a poem that nobody likes a wet dog.
Today I yell back at Billy:
"I love a wet dog."

I love a well-mannered,
shampooed, groomed,
clean, washed, wet dog.

I love a wet dog,
who keeps up with his hygiene,
dog paddling every few days
in a clean stream,
or taking a warm shower weekly.

My own dog
refuses to approach bodies of water.
For the eight years I have known him
he's a coward at the hiss of a hose,
not the dog you want
representing at the fire station.

He dropped out
of the personal grooming program at Petsmart.
His first, also last, groomer
called my phone two minutes after I left their parking lot.
She insisted I return to pick up a dry dirty dog,
who had turned surly
at the shampoo station in front of the doggy shower.

Years later,
his coat, black merging to brown,
where he lies on the ground, ombre
with a few detached sticks
the backyard cottonwood tree offered him.

Like Pigpen in Peanuts,
clothed in his own personal dust storm.
Dust that he, and he alone, likes.
Every season a little dustier.
Sometimes the new dust knocks off the old dust.
He likes to drop off a load in the kitchen
when I'm cooking.

He refuses to reveal his reasons
for staying dry and dirty.
A dog of mystery:
Perhaps his parents hail from
small towns in New Mexico,
Carrizozo or Claunch,
overly cautioning their puppy
about the dangers of rainstorms.
They avoided the ooze of overly watered lawns.
No swimming in arroyos,
They took him for memorable puppy walks
in xeriscaped drylands,
and overdid
pushing the joys of low-water usage.

The Sort-Of Stay-At-Home Dog

At the divorce, the husband
who built the house, kept the house,
I, who had adopted the dog,
kept the dog.
A moving truck deposited me
and my grief counselor in new quarters—
a backyard and a doggie door
leading to a kitchen
and a house full of boxes.

A family diaspora ensued:
children flowed away to adult lives,
the loyal dog continued to stay,
roaming between the backyard and the kitchen.
Cheerleading our move,
he inaugurated the moving van with one leg,
the backyard perimeters
with two legs.
New neighbors he greeted
with a friendly tail.
As we explored new walks, unknown bushes,
my friend towed me back to life,
showing me life after divorce
as a series of walks in the park.

Then suddenly, a few months after the move,
our new family unit came under fire,
by him, a reluctant runaway
who learned to jump the backyard wall.

Eleven times he leaped:
each time returning to the front door.
So impressed by his own feat,
that he needed to share the escape.
Surprised to be out,
wanting to come home again
"Are you my homie,
Or newly homeless?" I asked.

The twelfth time,
he was stuck inside a nearby gated subdivision.
I listened as he, on one side of a locked gate,
implored me to take him home,
once again.

The next day an electronic stay-at-home collar
shockingly clarified
the difference between jump and stay
and allowed him to continue being a homeboy.

The once-again stay-at-home dog
with less over-the-wall drama.

Random Daily Conversations On our Dog Walks

I thought we agreed:
No more aggressive moves on the ducks,
those mallards who don't make eye contact with us—
for good reason.

Remember:
our **no-bolting** pact?
I'm particularly opposed to the running vault
that spins me skittering off-kilter.
Surely, you've connected the dots:
More impulsivity, less dog biscuits.

Incidentally,
I'm over late-night barking at raccoons
in our backyard cottonwood tree:
You need your eight hours of dog-dream sleep,
as do I.

Furthermore,
you know how I feel about
growling at labradoodles.
Explain to me how the Chihuahua clan
rates high-fives,
and the poodle posse gets no respect.

By the way:
the first pee of the morning
should not land on our neighbor's white roses,
nor, at New Year's, on anyone's new white snowman.

Dare I remind you
of our pledge to ignore Yorkshire yippers
whose joy it is to challenge you.

And if I were you:
I wouldn't mad-dog the coyotes crossing our path.
Note their sharp teeth and hungry looks.

I hope you will remember to remember:
that skunks, rattlesnakes and porcupines
are not worth the bother.

Also, I've meant to tell you
it's NOT cool when you escape through the front door
and taunt me with your liberty.

Could we agree that
even if you are an above-average lab,
with a nice butt,
—who is *temporarily* free—
twerking is not attractive?

I know it's taxing to remember these rules,
but there are the perks of pet life:
breakfast, dinner
someone to scratch you
and our walk.
You know,
the walk with all the rules.

Letter of Apology to My Sleep-Deprived Neighbor

It was not my choice
that, pursuing a backyard raccoon,
my dog used his outdoor voice
late last night
under the tree, near your window,
barking until his voice roughened
but did not diminish in volume.

It was not my choice
he took a tough stand
on the issue of raccoons—
once and for all—
and resisted being dragged inside,
escaping my grip,
despite my request that
he sleep on the situation,
despite my suggestion that he might want to
tackle the raccoon problem
in the morning
with fresh eyes and a morning voice.

It was not my choice
he tried to outwait the raccoon;
I know raccoons
never follow orders and
always slip out of backyard trees
at breakfast time
when the coast is clear.

It was not my choice
to yell at him
after the first futile minutes of whispering to him,
which as you unfortunately know
escalated to talking,
then singing,
then screaming at him.

It probably was not your choice
to hear the blending of voices
between my dog and myself,
as we chorused back and forth,
in irritation,
me at him,
he at the raccoon,
both of us,
in an unsuccessful
tone of voice,
that was of our choosing
but hardly a good choice.

Despite our bad choices,
I would recommend
we blame the raccoon, that rascal!
for the neighborhood mayhem
that may have deprived you
of sleep, last night, all night.

A Dog's Dog

He was a dog's dog:
always ready to brawl
with raccoons.

Avidly on the look-out
for a mad-dog look
from another mutt
that required action: a punch,
bite, or a big-dog growl, at the least.

Muscular in his attention
to any situation
that involves
felines.

Always ready to
take a selfie
at any hydrant

Always ready for a mid-day nap and supper,
begged, stolen off the counter
or rightfully given.

2

Dog sense:

Doggerel about me becoming less dogmatic and more dog friendly

Dog Scents

There is morning magic
to be sniffed out in the bosque.
Invisible particles blanket the sage bush,
imparting sacred texts
into the nose of
my canine.

Firmly nosing
his way through bushes,
this dog is assaulted by messages
that say, "Read me first":

"Help me, I'm a big dog with a small bladder.
I'm running out of pee"
from a Jack Russell terrier.

Or, "Curses on you and all your kin;
"I'm glad I'm not a kept pet"
from the maw of a coyote
directly delivered through his urinary gland.

"Anyone interested in *knowing* me,
a six-year-old Pomeranian with great hair"
reads the want-ad of a flirt,
"Come bark at my house on Trellis and Vine."

My dog is an expert
at decoding complex canine inscriptions.
Sometimes he peels
away four layers of recent updates
on one much-messaged shrub.

While he focuses on hidden meanings,
threats, innuendos, invitations to brunch,
my job is to keep a visual lookout for dangers.
Like: is that a charcoal poodle in heat,
headed in our direction?

His canine brain is wired for synesthesia,
translating smell to action,
but I am hopeless with print
sprayed onto a plant,
despite hours logged
in the bushes with my dog.

When he smells enough messages
from those who walked before us,
he is ready to leave his own mark.

Just in case the next dog might miss him,
there is my dog, spraying,
respraying nearby plants,
then digging nearby dirt to broadcast
a message, some wisdom.
So that *his* meaning will not be lost.

Alternative-economy Jobs My Dog Is Eligible For

Bounty hunter for raccoons.
Excavator
of garden beds too small for backhoes.

Life-coach pulling
curmudgeons from couches
and out to walk in winter.

Pest-and-rodent eradicator,
monitoring your house perimeter
obsessively until the mice move next door.

Meet-and-greet specialist, at your Christmas party.
When you don't have time to chitchat with all,
he will lick their hands (and plates),
nudge their crotches,
provide unwonted entertainment.

 Home security engineer,
and active investigator
of rowdy raccoons.

Cheese taster:
happy to dispose of any brie
he can see on the counter.

Curfew enforcer:
he will send teenager
party raccoons packing.

Pacer on hiking trips:
he, who loves to walk,
will stop,
refuse to budge,
when you should be tired.

Karaoke singer in the backyard, at night;
doesn't need a song machine.

Paid proboscis
to sniff out the raccoons
living inside your cottonwood.

Neighborhood dogs-on-leashes enforcer,
strong sense of justice about the immorality
of unleashed doglife.

This employee
brings his own undeviating ethical sensibility
to the workplace.

Son of the Sun

Every morning a doggie door opens;
out bounds my canine
to execute an upward-facing dog,
salute the sun,
and water
his favorite tree.

My dog Cedro is a
temperature mongerer.
Like Apollo and his golden chariot,
he follows the arc of the sun
around our backyard.

As if part Aztec priest,
he knows where the sun hits
at 12:32 on January 21;
he is there,
gloriously snoring,
like the Emperor Montezuma.

At 2 pm, under the western portal,
he is once again
sleeping, twitching,
comfortably sunny
with a hint of shade.

When the doorbell rings
he abandons sun salutations
for indoor pettings,
before returning to the rigors
of radiant relaxation.

During summer middays
he hides his furry frame under eaves,
behind benches, under benches,
atop watered flowers.

Despite global warming
this black-coated
climatologist continues
a creative napping,
beneath leaking hoses and overturned chairs.

My homeboy
has made his
contribution
to global cooling.

Lie on wet dirt,
he models,
optimistically.

Dogs Who Love the Garden

Few gardeners are actual canines;
few canines are real gardeners.
A gifted puppy might
unintentionally scratch up a weed
or two,
but never all the tumbleweeds
he planted last year
in a joyous burst of excavation.

Burying his bone,
that digger helpfully
aerates the soil
around the trumpet vine.
Looking for that bone in the compost pile,
he stirs up beneficial enzymes,
but not without strewing
half composted bok choy
over garden paths.

While trailing a human gardener,
your average canine will stand on the furrow,
right where you have just planted
exquisite heirloom tomatoes,
and quizzically look into your eyes.
A not-irresistible
"Do you still love me,
while I am standing on the seedlings?"
sort of look.

A dog-loving gardener responds:
"I love you, I love the garden,
but I don't love you IN the garden."

Some Watchdog

For many years untested,
the assumption was
my macho black lab--
the one with the deep growl,
and surly snarl at other male dogs,
the dog who nipped a toddler
entering his personal space
would *certainly* cut a chunk from a robber's leg,
if that leg invaded our home.

But how to prove that theory?
I didn't want to invite a robber
over for a trial bite.
My canine burglar alarm continued to
snarl, bark, growl
and try to bite on our walks,
but remained untested at home.

Until last summer two friends, father and son,
unknown to the watchdog
came to visit the house.
Due to arrive before I returned,   I
I left them a key.
I locked my dog in the backyard,
warned them to leave the doggie door closed!
"Be careful of that dog— he's an aggressive guardian."

When they arrived,
he licked the door until they opened it,
greeted them as long last friends

with wet hugs and big kisses,
would have shown them where the silver was hidden
had they but asked.
When I got home it was Haight Ashbury anew,
with his love floating in the air.

Now I have a security system
that is electronic.

To serve

Like a man who reluctantly
dons a suit and tie
to work at the bank,
my dog agrees to wear a collar and leash
if *I* agree to walk him every day.

He agrees to eat dogfood,
although he would prefer steak.
He stays off the sofa when I am at home,
but sofa rules go missing, when I'm gone.
If I scratch him behind the ears for ten minutes,
he lets me knit in peace for a quarter hour.

If I close the dog door,
he agrees not to pry it open
using his nose as a lever,
unless there is a true emergency,
like the raccoon
waltzing in our backyard.

I've agreed not to insult him,
with phrases like: "Dogs will be dogs."
or "It's hard to teach an old dog new tricks"
I also try not to make fun of him,
by asking him when he's quiet,
"What's the matter, the cat got your tongue?"

I comfort him
during frightening times,
like the 4th of July
and he notes my need for personal space,
if I insist
(and I do.)

Often understanding
is lost in translation:
despite many gentle words, harsh ones and spankings,
he still forgets
and sleeps right on top
of the young Maximilian sunflowers.

Saved

Five years ago
when I moved to Spain for a year
I tried to give my dog away,
unsuccessfully.

The no-kill shelter was filled.
He, who was raised in the pound
would have despaired to return there.
I couldn't do that to him, so
no pound.

I put his best photo on a flier
begging a good person to take him;
however,
no dice.

I put an ad on Craig's List,
focusing on his finest points, but
nothing.

I talked to my friends
who don't have dogs
about the mental health pluses
of dog ownership.
No takers.

Then Jeannie, my house renter said,
"Leave the dog in the backyard."
and he was saved, just like that.

One year later, after Spain
when I greeted him, he wagged his tail
and looked at me quizzically, as if to say,
"You know me and my dog sense of time...
I think you were gone for a weekend.
Welcome back."

The Bicycling Canine

On cold, sleeting days,
if my dog and I skip our walk,
he fits in an indoor walk.

Right there in the kitchen,
he is off and running,
all the while napping.

His eyes fastened shut,
he bicycles four legs
in full pursuit of a wily raccoon.

Raccoon caught,
he deliriously drifts
into a vinyasa routine.

Then minutes later
pumps his twitching legs
back up into a high-speed chase
of more randy raccoons,
or preening porcupines
or is it terrorizing tomcats?

A multi-tasking sleeper,
he saves the neighborhood,
exorcises the bad guys,
and tones his calves
if left alone to nap.

Meanwhile I am *backpedaling*
about whether I have time

for the gym today.
I wish, like him, I could exercise
in a snoring position.

Obedience School Candidates

I was new to boyfriends.
I didn't realize that
He who let his dogs sleep on the sofa
at my house,
He, who helped the mutts
climb up on my bed
—despite MY protests—
was not the
top-dog, for me.

My dog,
loyal to me,
even argued with
his dogs, against his own interests.
In this scrappy dogfight,
confusion reigned between
many princes
and one queen.

I now know
that no-dogs-on-sofas
is not negotiable;
that a boyfriend without dog boundaries
gets the doggie door
right away;
he gets no
lap time.

The Humongous Scary Five-Foot Gopher Snake in the Backyard

A motionless snake in the backyard.
The motionless snake appeared dead.
The dead snake rubber?
The rubber snake a practical joke?
The joke really lifeless?
The lifeless snake a facsimile of a real rattler?
The facsimile really not moving
Or did I just see it twitch?

A snake *probably* no longer moving in the backyard.
WHAT IS IT DOING THERE?
Two puncture wounds on its chest look familiar,
like my dog's canine teeth.

My dog disavows knowledge
of these wounds, of this snake.
My dog has been snakeproofed at obedience school.
A snakeproofed dog is scared of snakes.
My supposedly-scared-of-snakes dog
feigns ignorance of our backyard snake.

But he doggedly shares this thought:
we do not want to approach
the lifeless, rubber, facsimile of a snake!
—just in case.

3

The Dog Days of his Wintering

Aging Out of the Fighting Life

My black attack-lab puppy is growing up.
He's nine.
No math whiz,
he confused the dog-years algorithm,
and lingered in his adolescence
far too many years,
jumping the backyard wall on a bad hip,
rushing feral cats, attacking mallards
longer than nine out of ten
orthopedic veterinarians recommended.

No longer able to play the puppy
who turns other male dogs into chew toys,
today a cautionary thought-flicker
precedes a lunge.

He forgets momentarily
that he is alpha male.
His learning curve
allows him that second of reflection.
He sees that treed racoons are *not* taunting him,
that the cats are ever younger, faster.

This mixed lab, mixed-up lab
has taken more years than expected
to take a day off from the chase—
then only when his hip is stiff.

Ode to My Dying Dog

Noble Cedro,
neutered refugee from the Eastside pound,
young landless prince of unknown nobility,
now king of a bosque backyard,
400 square feet,with a dog door to the kitchen
where your dish filled with dogfood awaits you.

Today you prepare for your final walk.
Cancer grips your heart and lungs;
you concentrate on breathing,
sleeping, slipping away.

You look distantly
when I try to feed you steak, hotdogs,
if only you would eat.

You still enjoy a walk in the bosque
with its so many familiar and mysterious smells
of dogs, ducks and coyotes.
But you labor to climb a small hillock
you bounded over last month.
Now you are canting,
panting, stopping, cannoting
not cantering.

Oh, to turn back the wings of time
which aged you seven years, to my one:
such a quick equation of vicious finality.

Oh, to revive those bosque sage bushes
you loved to roll in,
before the county mowers rashly razed them.

Oh, to finish off all the ducks,
who tried to waddle your same path.

Oh, to return to the grudges,
growls and barks of yesteryear,
liberally sprinkled upon the poodles
repeatedly, repetitively on the raccoons of the hood.

The memory of that barking is music,
in the face of your rattled breathing.

Happily you outlasted the neighbor dogs,
unruly Molly and Greta
who moved away last week;
perhaps their crime of unleashed exuberance
can now be forgiven.

Yes, I say,
all is forgiven:
the digging,
secret sleeping on the couch,
obsessive pacing at night
when the raccoons were maurading
and your doggie door was firmly locked.
Even the six am barking can now be forgotten.

Our bosque walks will continue
with you strangely missing.

There will be less pollination of your favorite sages.
fewer goatheads strewn from your paws
across the bikepath.
The coyotes will notice the quiet,
and the ducks on river sandbars
will no longer be startled by your sudden presence.

You, my friend, will be missed.

Someone Tell the Neighborhood Birds

Someone tell the neighborhood birds
that the fierce dog
who protected his backyard with passion
has left us.

It is safe for them to visit
the backyard bird feeder
once again.

To Tattoo?

In the dogdays of my pet's dying season,
I look at the wintering of my muse,
the suddenly graying dog at my feet.

He was that dog who would live forever,
so full of good cheer
and lively immortality.

For eight years, he awoke
with delight at day's dawning;
his exuberance a gift to me.

He leaves no progeny;
spayed at the pound before
I could preserve His Graciousness
in a puppy.

Now dogless after his death
I wonder how to hold my muse close:
whether
to get his tattoo,
or not to.

I do not want such a great dog
to disappear;
every inch of me wants to
preserve every inch of him.

Can a tattoo commemorate
his courage and nobility?
A needleful of ink
preserve his soulful eyes?

Or do justice to his ankle, so delicate,
yet strong enough to lift him, as if winged,
over the backyard wall?

Would a tattoo
remind me
love is permanent,
let my muse
inspire me, still?

Holes Dug By His Holiness

The canine renovation
of the backyard stopped
holefully incomplete,
when the architect,
my digging dog, died.

Now, seven pounds of
rawhide bones--
buried in secret places--
could be sold as scrap
and holes filled in.

Yet it is unholy
to undo the hard work
of a good dog.

Megan Baldrige is an Albuquerque poet who was lucky enough to live with a wonderfully challenging, fun Black Lab named Cedro. They used to walk the walk, without really being able to agree on either the walk or the talk. After lots of advice from well-meaning family members and several bouts of obedience school, they agreed to agree to agree whenever that was possible and to pretend to agree the rest of the time.

Jules' Poetry Playhouse Publications is a division of Jules' Poetry Playhouse, LLC founded by Jules Nyquist in 2012 in Albuquerque, New Mexico. My publishing mission grew out of requests to record collaborations in poetry and art in book form so that we may realize our common bonds and to provide community support as readers and writers. www.julesnyquist.com

81463807R00038

Made in the USA
Columbia, SC
01 December 2017